LOVE MADE THE DIFFERENCE

Helen Temple Classics

LOVE MADE THE THE DIFFERENCE
HELEN TEMPLE

Beacon Hill Press of Kansas City
Kansas City, Missouri

Copyright 2003
by Beacon Hill Press of Kansas City

ISBN 083-412-0429

Printed in the
United States of America

Cover Design: Paul Franitza

All Scripture quotations not otherwise designated are from the
King James Version.

Library of Congress Cataloging-in-Publication Data

Temple, Helen, 1914-
  Love made the difference / Helen Temple.
      p. cm. — (Helen Temple classics)
    ISBN 0-8341-2042-9
  1. Missionaries—Biography. 2. Love—Religious aspects—Christianity.
I. Title. II. Series: Temple, Helen, 1914-, Helen Temple classics.

  BV3700.T44 2003
  266'.023—dc21

                                                    2002156569

10   9   8   7   6   5   4   3   2   1

CONTENTS

ABOUT THE AUTHOR

HELEN TEMPLE—the most prolific author of mission books in the history of the Church of the Nazarene—has more than 60 titles to her credit (40-plus for adults/youth and 20-plus for children). From 1951 to 1985, she authored one or more books annually. All the more remarkable is the fact that she served as an editor for the World Mission Division for 32 years, most of that time as editor of the *Other Sheep* magazine.

Even in retirement, Miss Temple's pen remains active. Her most recent book is *Adventure with God: The Jeanine van Beek Story,* published by Beacon Hill Press in 2002. For the 2001-2005 quadrennium, she has been commissioned to prepare the Helen Temple Classics series, a collection of her best writings, which will include one book per year.

During the last half of the 20th century, and now in the third millennium, Nazarenes appreciate and value Helen Temple for her gift in bringing missions into their homes and hearts. Truly, Helen Temple is a beloved author and devoted servant of the Lord with an irrefutable passion for missions.

INTRODUCTION

THESE STORIES, taken from books written in the 1950s and 1960s, are an ageless record of the love of God revealed in the lives of ordinary people.

Three people, in widely separated parts of the world, reached out to those in need with the gift of the One who loved us all. In widely divergent ways they say the same thing: "The love of Christ constraineth us" (2 Corinthians 5:14).

Whether it is a love that plants the gospel to spread across a continent or changes a village or a single life, the cup of water given in Christ's name transforms the lives of those it touches.

Just so simply Christ planned His conquest of the world.

As you read, may you also be impelled to reach out with your gift of His love to someone who is hurting and become a vital part of His ongoing story.

SMOKE FROM A THOUSAND VILLAGES

IT WAS EARLY SPRING in Texas. The warm languid air was filled with the fragrance of flowers and the lazy hum of bees. Most of the students at Peniel College dozed or chatted lazily as they sprawled on the new grass, soaking in the sunshine.

But one young man was inside his room. He stared unseeing at the blurred lines of print. The last words he had read stood out like a glaring light: "I have sometimes seen, in the morning sun, the smoke of a thousand villages where no missionary has ever been."*

A thousand villages without Christ! These were the words of Robert Moffatt that had sent David Livingstone out to die in Africa. Now they were calling to Harmon Schmelzenbach.

---

*The book being read was possibly *The Personal Life of David Livingstone,* by W. G. Blaikie, London: Murray, 1880.

11

He dropped to his knees and wept as he cried out in anguish, "Lord, here am I. Send me to tell them."

The burden never lessened. Finally, unable to bear the strain of waiting to finish school, Harmon decided to leave without telling anyone of his plans.

Secrets are not easily kept in a small college like Peniel, however, and his preparations to leave were soon discovered. A farewell service was held in his honor the next Sunday evening. Under the waves of blessing that flowed over the congregation that night, the students and teachers pledged their prayers and $200 a year for five years for Harmon's support.

As soon as Harmon had raised sufficient money for his passage, he packed his few belongings and headed for New York.

Entering the New York Steamship Company office on May 1, 1907, Harmon glanced curiously at the eight other travelers who were there as he was— to secure tickets to Africa. There were five single women, a married couple, a young man, and an older woman, chaperoning the single ladies.

The voyage was pleasant, uneventful, and, to Harmon, unending. But though eager to be at his calling, he knew that he must first find some group with whom to work while he learned one of the many African languages.

He found a place with an independent faith mission in Port Elizabeth and began to study the Xhosa language, only mildly aware that two of the young ladies who had been on the ship were also working with the same mission. Gradually he became aware that Lula Glatzel was an attractive and interesting person. When the two young people recognized their growing interest in each other, they both prayed earnestly about it, for neither had expected that there would be any possibility of marriage when they answered God's call to a pagan land.

Assured of God's will, they were married on June 19, 1908, one year and a day after their arrival in Africa.

Their first assignment together came almost at once—a strange honeymoon indeed. "We need a married couple at our station in Pondoland," the mission director said. "Will you go?"

They accepted the appointment eagerly and left immediately for Port John. From there they traveled by oxcart a hundred miles over bumpy, rutted roads—or no roads at all, which was sometimes better—until they reached the inland village of Bazana.

For three months they worked happily together, getting the mission established. Then one day they had a visitor. They recognized him as the government official in the area and were both flattered and nervous to be entertaining such a distinguished guest.

"What church do you represent?" the official asked casually, after they had visited for a while.

"We don't represent any denomination," Harmon answered. "We are working for the White Holiness Mission in Port Elizabeth. It is an independent faith mission."

"I see." The official was silent for a long moment. Then he said, "You know, I suppose, that you cannot operate a mission and live among the African people unless you represent a church body that is registered with the government. You may live in the European community in Bazana if you like, but we can't allow you to live here among the African people."

The Schmelzenbachs were stunned. The African people lived at least six miles from the European town. How could they work with them if they could not live in their community?

After much agonizing prayer, Harmon came to a painful decision: "We are wasting the Lord's time and money every day we stay here," he said to Lula. "We'd better go back to Durban."

With discouraged hearts, they packed their few belongings and hired a transport driver to take them to the nearest port where they could secure passage. At Durban they found in the poorer section of the city a little house they could afford to rent.

Harmon started out the next morning in search of an unevangelized section of the African community near the European center, where they could work. He came home discouraged.

"These Africans are Zulus," he said as he slumped in a chair. "I'll have to learn another new language."

The next day he purchased a Zulu grammar and dictionary and plunged into his study.

Now that they were settled in one spot, letters and papers from the United States began to catch up with them. From these they learned that Peniel College and the church there had joined the Pentecostal Church of the Nazarene in October 1907. Harmon was automatically a Nazarene. But was he their missionary too? They waited anxiously for a letter of confirmation.

In February 1909 the hoped for letter came from Dr. Ellyson in Kansas City. "You are now a Nazarene," the letter said, "and we will be glad to consider you our missionary if you decide to remain a Nazarene. Would you consider opening a work in Durban for the church?"

They prayed much before answering his letter. But the many missions they had already seen in Durban convinced them that there was no way they could open a new mission without encroaching on territory already being evangelized by others.

At last Harmon wrote to Dr. Ellyson, "We have longed for the day when we might become missionaries for the Pentecostal Church of the Nazarene in Africa," Harmon wrote. "But we do not feel there is a great need for another mission here in Durban. Our purpose and burden for which we came here is to open work among people who are totally unevangelized. Could you help us get started in such a work?

It is our dream and, I believe, God's will and purpose in sending us to Africa."

With much prayer they posted their letter and waited anxiously for a reply.

Several months later the long awaited reply arrived. Eagerly they tore it open.

"We are sorry, but your proposal to search for unevangelized territory and establish a new work would require more funds than we have available at this time," they read with unbelieving eyes. It was hard to realize that the anticipated door had so suddenly closed in their faces.

"I am still convinced that God wants us to open work in some unevangelized area where no one else is working," Harmon said with conviction. "We have been marking time long enough. We will write our friends and tell them we are going to save any extra funds we get, and when we have enough, we will start out on our own to find the place God has for us."

Little by little the funds trickled in. Every penny they could possibly save they put away, until a year later they had accumulated $750. To the missionaries, it seemed like a magnificent amount.

"This is enough!" Harmon declared. "We'll start out."

"Where to?" Lula asked apprehensively, as she lifted their baby son in her arms.

"I'm not certain," Harmon answered. "I've been studying about the areas where they speak Zulu.

Swaziland is the most promising country. I don't think it has been wholly evangelized yet. We'll start in that direction and see how God leads."

Swaziland! That was 300 miles away! It had been an adventure to travel with her husband, earlier. But now with a baby the trip looked impossible. How would they travel? What would they eat? How would they know where to go?

A week after Harmon's decision to leave, Lula was roused by a shout from the outside. "Lula, come out a minute." It was her husband's voice. She hurried to the door and stopped in dismay. There he sat, smiling broadly, on the seat of a small wagon drawn by four of the smallest donkeys she had ever seen.

"Here's our home for the next few weeks," he said, climbing down.

Lula looked dubious. The wagon seemed far too small to hold a third of their belongings. And the donkeys! "Do you think those tiny creatures can pull that wagon when it's loaded?" she asked.

He laughed. "They're very strong. The Dutch farmers use them all the time. I'll build a framework over the top and cover it with canvas. Then I'll put in two bunks and pack our goods in and around them. We'll be dry and comfortable and probably safer from snakes and insects than we are right here."

Now that the decision had been made to go, Harmon was anxious to be on his way. A Zulu boy, to whom some unlinguistic white man had given the name of Billy, was hired to be their driver, interpreter, guide, and goodwill ambassador to the communities through which they would pass. There would be government stations here and there along the way, and they would have to depend upon these for replenishing their food stocks, for they could not carry enough to take them through.

They wrote the South African Inland Mission of their plans, and as soon as their replacement missionaries arrived, they were ready to leave.

Early in the morning on October 3, 1910, they left Durban for what they fervently hoped would be their last journey.

The country they traveled through was rough and hilly. Sometimes there were crude roads, sometimes not. A map of sorts offered them a general guide; their faith in God supplied the rest, as they rode slowly across the African countryside. With the need to stop early to let the donkeys rest and graze, they felt fortunate indeed if they could cover as much as five miles in a day, which they often did not.

Week after week dragged by, filled with the monotony of the rattling, jouncing cart and the roadside stops for food and rest. Yet slowly, steadily, they drew nearer to the land they were seeking.

God did indeed take care of the little family and brought them through the wilderness to Mankayane, a southern district of Swaziland.

Here they found a mission station of the South

Africa General Mission. They stayed there for a few days, talking long and fervently with their hosts, asking about possible areas of the country where no missions were working.

"There are one or two missions working not too far from us," was the reply, "but the northern part of Swaziland has no missionaries as far as we know. The people speak Zulu."

Harmon smiled at Lula. "This sounds like our dream, at last," he said.

While Lula and Little David stayed at the mission, Harmon went on ahead to find a suitable place to establish a new mission.

As he walked through the country, he was both impressed and burdened since he saw no sign of a mission station or of any missionaries working anywhere. This looked more and more like the place he had been longing to find. At last he came into central Swaziland and the Pigg's Peak district. At Pigg's Peak he called on the government commissioner and explained his purpose in coming.

"We're glad to have you," the commissioner answered cordially, "and certainly these people need a mission. But you had better go and get your family right away. The rainy season will begin any day now, and when it does, the rivers will all be in flood and you will not be able to get in here at all."

Harmon hastened to make the long trip home and report on his good fortune. Hurriedly he and

Lula assembled food supplies, bade their mission hosts good-bye, and set out for the last trek of their long journey. Within a few hours, they were at the descent of the Usutu Mountains.

One look at the steep, rocky, downward trail, and Lula scrambled from the wagon with David. "I'll walk!" she said decisively. "I think it will be safer."

Picking her way over the boulder-strewn and sometimes slippery trail, she followed the careening wagon down the mountain.

At the bottom she looked with dismay at the tumbled heap of things that had once been their neatly packed belongings.

"This is the hardest part of the trip, I think," Harmon comforted her as she began to repack the wagon. "From here on we ought to be able to make it all right."

The wagon rolled on easily on the gentle slope that led to the river. But at its banks they stopped in dismay. The Usutu was already flooding—200 feet across its shallow bed and eating hungrily at the bank where they would have to enter.

"Should we wait a few hours for it to go down?" Harmon asked his driver.

Billy shook his head. "This means the rains have begun up north," he said. "In a few days no one will cross the river. If you want to go, you will have to go now."

Lula was fearful. "Do you think we should try to

cross?" she asked anxiously, holding her small son tight in her arms.

"We have to," Harmon answered. "We can't stay here, and we've no other way to go. You climb up on the seat and hold the baby. Hang on with all your strength, and pray." There was no need to remind her to pray. Lula had never stopped praying since they had left the mountaintop.

While Billy drove, Harmon waded into the stream guiding the donkeys. The little wagon lurched forward, bouncing and staggering over the rocky riverbed. Thirty yards out in the now swiftly flowing stream, the wheels suddenly sagged into a bed of sand and stopped. Anxiously Harmon coaxed and shouted at the donkeys, but they could not move the wagon. They leaned back into the harness and suddenly, without warning, the wheel donkey lay down in the river. Frantically Harmon caught at its bridle and pulled the animal's head above water. One of the lead donkeys promptly disappeared beneath the water, and the missionary had to drag him to his feet. No sooner had he pulled these two up than the other two went down.

Billy waded around to help him.

They could not turn the wagon around, nor back it up. Unless they could get the donkeys to move ahead and soon, they would all be under the water and the wagon too.

In the midst of their despair they heard a shout

from the far side of the river. An Afrikaner, on his way to Mbabane, had come to the crossing and, seeing their plight, unhitched his mules and drove them into the rushing stream.

Hitching his fresh team quickly to the front of the donkeys, he pulled them all safely to shore on the other side.

Gratefully the exhausted missionaries thanked him for his help.

"It is nothing," he answered, with a wave of his hand. "But you are new in this country, I can see. One thing you must always remember. Never, never try to cross a river with tired donkeys. They will always try to drown themselves."

The weary travelers rested for a while beside the river, then started on their way. Every hour counted now, for if the rains had begun in the mountains to the north, every river in the area would be flooding and they might be stranded in the wilderness with no food.

They reached Mbabane, the capital of Swaziland, in a few days and stopped at the little settlement of Europeans long enough to rest and replenish their supplies.

"Where are you going?" the people asked, eyeing the dusty, mud-stained wagon.

"To Pigg's Peak," answered Harmon, with a confidence born of the conviction that this was where God was directing them.

Their new friends looked apprehensive. "You'll never get across the Komati," said one. "It's the worst river in this part of Africa, and it's already beginning to flood. You'd better plan to stay here until the rainy season is over."

"We can't possibly do that," Harmon replied, thinking of their dwindling savings.

"You know, don't you," one said, "that you may not be able to enter the northern territory of Swaziland? The queen has not allowed any new settlers to locate in her area for 12 years or more."

For the first time despair struck the hearts of the weary travelers. Had they come all this way in vain?

Disturbed and saddened by this latest news, they nevertheless continued their preparations to leave. The following day they hitched up the donkeys and began the rugged climb up the mountain trail.

Two days later they reached the banks of the dreaded Komati River. True to prediction, the broad, swift-flowing stream was in flood. It would be impossible to cross it with the wagon.

With Billy as their mediator, they negotiated with some Swazi men who were standing by the river. Eventually they agreed that if the missionaries would take the wagon apart and let the men carry it and its contents across piece by piece, the Swazi men would transport them and their belongings across the river. It sounded precarious, but it was the only possible way they could get across.

Everything had to be unloaded from the wagon, the wagon taken totally apart, and then everything carried across piece by piece to the other side. There it had to be reassembled, and all the contents reloaded.

By the time they had finished, the day was far-gone. There was nothing to do but spend the night on higher ground a short distance from the river.

They were already two days longer on the trail than they had intended, and there had been no government station for many miles.

That noon when they stopped to rest and let the donkeys graze, they cooked the last of the mealies (corn meal) into porridge and fed the baby. He wept hungrily until he fell into an exhausted sleep.

Late in the afternoon, a low rumble of thunder sounded behind them. They looked back to see heavy clouds rolling down over the mountains. There was just time to reach the partial shelter of a small hill when hailstones began to fall. Tying the donkeys hastily to a tree in the lee of the hill, Harmon and Billy crept into the wagon with the family. Part of the cover tore loose from the wagon, and soon their goods were a sodden shambles.

Wrapping the baby in blankets, Lula held him in her arms, shielding him as best she could from the driving rain and hail.

Darkness fell as the storm ended, and they spent the night huddled together in the drenched wagon.

The sun came out bright and clear the next

morning, and they crept from their sodden shelter to survey the damage. Horrified, they gazed at the trail on which they had spent the night. Scarcely a foot from the wagon wheels, the edge of the road dropped off, sheer and straight, a hundred feet down into the valley below.

With grateful hearts they drove the donkeys ahead to a safe place, and they proceeded to unpack everything and spread it out to dry in the hot African sun. Night came before they had completed repacking their dried possessions.

At dawn they hitched up the donkeys and started on. It was a long day. Lula, Harmon, and Billy were faint from hunger. Their hearts were torn by the wails of the hungry baby. But the day ended, and darkness fell without any sign of the Peak.

Again they camped beside the trail for the night and set out at break of day.

"It can't be much farther," Harmon said desperately. "I know we must be close to Pigg's Peak."

As the long day was ending, they rounded a turn and saw the magistrate's office just ahead. Lula wept with relief.

"Stop and rest," the magistrate invited cheerily. "You look all in. Have you had a bad trip?"

"Rough but not impossible," Harmon answered. "Our supplies are a bit low, though. It took us longer than we expected. Is there any place in the vicinity where we can buy supplies?"

"Yes, there's a little store about a mile up the road."

While Billy unhitched the donkeys and put them to graze, Harmon walked to the store. Lula tried in vain to quiet the crying baby.

The magistrate's wife heard his cries and hurried out. "Is your baby ill?" she asked with concern.

"No, he's just hungry," Lula answered, embarrassed. "We were longer on the way than we expected, and we ran out of food."

"Why, you poor dear!" exclaimed the magistrate's wife. "And you haven't had anything to eat either, I know. I'll fix something right away."

She was gone before Lula could protest and soon was back with a basket of food.

As they talked with the commissioner that evening, he said, "You would do well to go to Endzingeni. There is a house there, and if you can get permission from the queen to settle in the country, you could very likely live in the house. We can't guarantee what the queen will say, but the British government is willing for you to locate here for mission work."

Four days of rest revived the tired donkeys and the travelers. With eager anticipation they set out on the last 15 miles of their month's long journey. Three days later they glimpsed the house in Endzingeni, only, to their dismay, to discover that it was already occupied. Hesitantly the missionaries explained to the Europeans why they were there.

The people were cordial. "You are welcome," they said. "You can move into the extra room here until you find out whether the queen will let you stay. We'll move on if she gives you permission to work here."

The one room seemed wonderfully spacious after the cramped little wagon.

By the next week Harmon was anxious to make the 15-mile trek back to the commissioner's headquarters to learn of the queen's decision.

He left at the first sign of dawn, full of hope, but when he returned that evening, his step was heavy, and Lula knew he did not have good news.

"What is wrong?" she asked anxiously. "Has the queen said we can't stay here?"

"No," Harmon answered, sighing. "It's the house. The commissioner says we aren't allowed to live in the house until the queen gives her permission for us to settle here. We have to move back into the wagon."

Lula stared at him wordlessly. Never had the one room seemed so pleasant as it did at that moment.

Mechanically they repacked their boxes, and Harmon carried them back and put them under the bunks and into the corners of the little wagon. And there they stayed for eight long months waiting for word from the queen of the Swazis.

Billy picked up rumors that the Zulu headmen were not pleased with the coming of the white man.

Then they heard that the high commissioner of Swaziland was privately interceding with the queen, and she seemed to be leaning with favor to their coming.

A few weeks later came the joyful news that the queen had given her permission for the Schmelzenbachs to settle in her country and open a mission.

With eager anticipation, Harmon started out at once, walking to the nearest kraals [pronounced "crawls," which means "homes"] to tell the Swazis of the God who loved them. To his dismay, they fled at his coming.

In the weeks that followed, as he and Lula walked the paths from kraal to kraal, the response was the same. They wanted none of his words and hid from sight whenever they approached.

Sitting at home after a weary day of tramping the trails, Harmon said thoughtfully, "I don't believe we'll ever convince these people we are their friends until we do something for them that they will understand. Tomorrow I am going to try something different. I'm going to take such medicine as I have and call only on those who have burns or other diseases that I can recognize and treat."

The next morning Harmon started out early. He went to a kraal where he knew there was an old man with a severe burn on his leg. Asking his permission, he knelt in the dust of the hut and cleaned the wound, applied his ointment to the burn, and wrapped the leg. Then he prayed earnestly for God to add His healing power and make the man well.

He went on his way to the next home where there was a person he thought he could help.

As he returned, day after day, and the sick began to get well, he sensed the respect of the Swazis growing, but they would not listen to his message of a God who loved them. For 18 months he walked the trails of Swaziland, helping the sick and talking of God, but no one responded.

Then one day as Harmon told the story once again in an old man's kraal, his young wife, Mangwane, suddenly spoke up boldly. "Umfundisi [Son of the King], I would be a believer if he would let me."

Angrily her husband turned to her. "You are starting a lie!" he cried. "This long time now you have been troubling me to become a believer in this white man's god. Only yesterday I told you that I would not be responsible for you in this matter. You know that the witch doctor has pronounced a curse on any who follow this way. If you wish to do so, you must take the trail alone."

Harmon spoke up quickly. "Do you mean that if your wife chooses to serve God, you will not trouble her?"

"Yes, Umfundisi, that is what I am telling her."

The missionary turned joyfully to the woman. "Did you hear what your husband said? You take the road with God, and he will not trouble you. Do you want to pray now?"

"No! No!" cried the old man fearfully. "Not in my kraal. Not before my eyes. If her heart is telling her to do this thing, let her go to your home and pray. Not here."

The woman began to weep. "Umfundisi, the day is nearly gone, and the trail to your house is long. I can't come today. But I will be there tomorrow, and I will become a believer in your God."

The missionaries slept little that night, thinking and praying for this first trembling soul on the threshold of decision.

The sun was scarcely up the next morning when a gentle cough at the door let them know that Mangwane was there. She was wearing the usual Swazi dress—a cowhide skirt, with a goatskin for a blouse. With her was her 10-year-old daughter. Mangwane's hair was woven with grass cords into a dome shape on the top of her head. Within, the missionary knew, were the usual witch doctor's fetishes, placed there when she was a small girl to protect her from harm.

The missionaries invited their visitors in. Mangwane and her daughter sat hesitantly on the floor, looking about them at the strange dwelling.

Reaching up to a low shelf, Lula took down a Testament and began looking for passages of Scripture she thought would help the woman.

Mangwane put out her hand, protesting.

"Inkosikasi [Daughter of the King], I do not want that this morning. I don't need it. You have told me the way many times. I believe every word. Today I want to know how I can have my sins forgiven. I want to be delivered from the power of the evil spirits.

Very simply, Harmon instructed her to pray after him the penitent's prayer for mercy and forgiveness. In a few moments she sat up and rubbed the tears from her face.

"It's all right, Umfundisi," she said smiling. "Jesus has come. My heart tells me so."

The missionaries began to give her some simple instructions, but she interrupted them. "I want a blue spell," she said, motioning to the blue, paper-covered Zulu primer lying on the table. She knew that before she could read the Bible, she would have to learn to read, and she had heard that this book would teach her.

"We will begin lessons this very day," Lula assured her.

"And I want a dress like yours. I want to look like a believer," she said.

Lula brought cloth from her cupboard and began to measure Mangwane and her little girl for simple dresses.

As she worked, Mangwane again surprised her. "Would you also give me a piece of soap to wash my hair?" she said.

The amazed missionaries were delighted to grant her request. These were standards they had not expected her to have the insight or courage to take up for weeks. Yet with the guidance of the Holy Spirit she had unerringly chosen to take her stand in a way that no one would mistake.

As the new Christian and her daughter left for the trip home, Harmon turned to Lula. In a voice full of emotion, he said, "One! We have led one to Jesus Christ! One, from a thousand villages that are without Christ. Maybe the ice of indifference has broken at last!"

But even with his great faith, he could not envision the spread of the gospel across Swaziland and beyond, to cover almost the entire African continent from coast to coast and from the Cape to the northernmost Islamic countries. Today there are more than 237,000 Nazarenes in Africa. And far more than a thousand villages in Africa know and love the name of Jesus Christ.

2

OLD ONE

"MADAMSAHIB, MADAMSAHIB," a faint quavery voice came from outside the missionary's cottage.

"Shall I answer the door?" asked the new missionary, starting to get up.

"No, there's no need. It's only Old One. Cook will give her a bit of food, and she will go away."

The older missionary sighed. "Poor thing! Her mind is so dulled by old age that she isn't able to grasp even the simplest truth. She can't work. We've tried to give her little tasks to do, but she can't even learn to sweep. Poor old woman!" She lifted her head and listened for a moment to the shuffling footsteps outside as they slowly made their way toward the kitchen.

"We feed her," she added, picking up her pen to resume her work, "but that seems to be all we can do."

The new missionary walked to the window and watched Old One as she painfully eased herself to a seat on the ground and hungrily ate the bowl of rice and curry the cook had given her.

Poor woman! the new missionary thought sadly. *So old, so near to the end of life and not able to understand that Jesus loves her!* She turned away, and a tear trickled down her cheek for Old One—and for the thousands of others in India who didn't know about Jesus.

A group of young Indian nurses came by, chattering gaily as they passed through the mission on their way to their duties at the hospital, their white saris (Indian dresses) fluttering in the light morning breeze.

"Namaste [Salutation to you], Old One," they greeted the old woman cheerily.

She looked up, pleased with their respectful attention. "Salaam, Missesahibs," she replied, using the older greeting that had been proper when she was a girl.

"Old One," one of the young nurses stopped suddenly before her. "Do you love Jesus?"

The old woman stared at her for a moment and then shook her head. "I don't know anyone by that name," she answered matter-of-factly.

"Come on, Sagunabai," the other nurses called, "you'll be late."

The girl smiled a friendly farewell and hurried after her friends.

"You shouldn't tease Old One, Sagunabai," one of the other nurses admonished. "She can't help it that her mind has dimmed with the years."

"I wasn't teasing her. I think Jesus could save her if we could just make her understand." Sagunabai nodded her head with earnest conviction.

The others laughed. "Sagunabai is being our little preacher again," they said. "Of course Old One
could be saved if we could make her understand, but
how do you propose to do that when the missionaries
have not been able to?"

Sagunabai did not smile. "She is a soul who
needs God," she said determinedly. I can't believe
that God would create people who need Him and
not make some way for them to understand that He
loves them."

Her eyes grew thoughtful. "Old One grew up in
the old ways of India," she said slowly. "Perhaps our
missionaries are not able to go back into those ways
far enough to approach her on paths she can understand."

They entered the hospital without answering,
suddenly sobered by Sagunabai's words.

Hospital hours were always busy, and the nurses
had time for only a fleeting smile or a word of greeting when they passed each other in the corridors, but
as soon as their duties were over, they gathered in a
cluster about Sagunabai.

"We have been thinking . . ." It was almost a
chorus so unanimous was their agreement. "We have
been thinking about what you said this morning, and
we think that perhaps you may be right. Have you
any ideas about how to reach Old One?"

Sagunabai looked surprised and pleased. "I have
been thinking too," she answered. "I don't know

how we can reach her, but I am going to try. Perhaps God will show us a way."

It was not hard to find Old One. She was too frail to wander far, and she had no home to go to. Since the mission area where she received a little food and shelter had a small outbuilding, it was the pleasantest place for her to be. She stayed there most of the time.

They found her sitting in the scant shade of the flame-of-the-forest tree, muttering to herself with her eyes closed against the glare of the afternoon sun.

"Salaam, Old One," they greeted her.

Startled by their sudden approach and the familiar greeting of her youth, she looked up quickly, her wrinkled face softening in welcome as she recognized them.

"Salaam, Missesahibs," she responded, smiling. "You speak the good words of the old days." For a moment Old One looked almost happy.

"The old days were good days, weren't they?" Sagunabai said gently.

"Not too bad—not too bad," Old One answered cautiously, fearful of seeming too eager lest the gods become jealous.

"Would you like to tell us about the good days when you were young?" one of the nurses added.

Old One brightened at their interest. It had been years since anyone had wanted to listen to anything she had to say. She straightened her ragged sari

with gnarled fingers. "When I was young, little ones
. . . ," she smiled and looked away to the far blue sky
beyond the mission wall, "when I was young, the village was a good place to live."

The young nurses looked at one another and
smiled, for they knew the village had always been
very much as it was today.

But the old woman went on, fancy and senti-
ment weaving their warm strands into her memories.
"I married when I was seven," she said dreamily. "I
had a rich dowry. And my husband gave me the most
beautiful sari for my wedding gown—gold and scarlet
threads drawn through it—and a blouse that was the
envy of the whole village . . ." Her voice wandered
off, and she was lost in her dreams of the past.

"Did you have children, Old One?" questioned
one of the nurses.

"Oh, yes . . . many children." She held up her
hands spreading her crooked fingers. "Twelve, 14—I
do not remember now." A shadow crossed her face.
"They died while still babies, all but 2, a son and a
daughter." She was lost again in retrospect.

"Old One," Sagunabai's voice was soft and gentle. "Let me read you a story about another Son, the
most wonderful Person the world has even known."
She opened her Bible and began to read the story of
the birth of Jesus.

The old woman listened attentively for a few
moments, then her eyes closed and she nodded, lost

in dreams of the days when she had been young and strong.

Quietly the nurses tiptoed away. "Do you think she heard anything you read?" one asked Sagunabai.

"Who can tell?" Sagunabai answered. "We must be patient. She is very old."

Daily the young nurses read the Bible to the old woman. Sometimes she seemed to listen with understanding, but often she would nod or break into their reading with long tales of her youth.

They always listened to her respectfully, hoping by their attention to build up a confidence that would give them an approach to her heart. Sagunabai, especially, listened intently whenever the woman told of her younger days, for the nurse still believed that somewhere in the old woman's memories she would find "an old path" that would lead her to believe in God.

"Tell us about your son, Old One," Sagunabai said one day. "Does he still live?"

The old woman sighed. "No, he, too, is gone. His spirit left his body before the last great famine."

Then the old mind drifted back to earlier days, and her face brightened.

"He was a beautiful child," she said proudly. "Strong, straight-limbed, sturdier than any child in the village. We were very proud of him, his father and I. We sent him to school. It was very costly, and not many village boys were able to go, but the headman had taken a fancy to him and wanted him to learn to read and write so that he could work for him. It was very unusual for one of our caste to be allowed to go to school," she smiled dreamily.

"And what then?" prompted Sagunabai. "Did your son work for the headman?"

"Ah, yes." Old One sat erect with pride as she remembered. "My son became the handler of all the headman's accounts and served him faithfully until he died from the fever before the last famine."

"You must have loved your son very much, Old One," Sagunabai said softly.

The old woman's face quivered with grief. "He was my only son," she answered simply. She brushed away a tear in embarrassment. "I am old and weak," she said half-angrily. Her voice dropped in despair. "There has been no one to care for me since he went. I am alone, and I am very old."

"Old One," Sagunabai leaned forward in her earnestness. "There is Someone who cares for you— Someone who also had an only Son. He loved you so much that He gave His only Son to die for you to pay the price for all your sins so that you could live with Him in heaven one day. We call Him God."

For a moment there was a flicker of response in the old woman's eyes.

Sagunabai pressed her advantage. "It would take a great love to be willing to give an only son for someone, do you not think so, Old One?"

"I could not do it," answered the old woman shaking her head.

"Do you understand how much God loves you when He would give His only Son to pay for your sins."

The old woman looked up, sudden understanding in her face and eyes. "You mean—God did that—for me?"

"For you," answered Sagunabai earnestly. "He died to provide forgiveness for your sins. Think how much He loved you."

"It is good," mumbled the old woman. "It is very good, but I don't understand. Let me think about it," and she closed her eyes.

"I think we are finding the way to her heart," rejoiced Sagunabai as the nurses left. "If only she will live long enough for God to penetrate her darkness with His light! We must pray harder."

Faithfully the little group of Indian nurses talked, read, and prayed with Old One whenever they had a free moment. Slowly, almost infinitesimally, the darkness was pushed back and the light crept into Old One's groping mind.

One day the old woman surprised the missionaries by asking them for a broom. Following the simple instructions of the patient Indian nurses, she learned to sweep, first the path, then the veranda of the hospital. The mastery of this first simple task encouraged her, and she began to learn to do other things by which she could earn her daily rice.

She listened to the preaching at church with growing understanding until at last her faith caught hold, and she opened her heart to receive God's forgiveness and His love.

New life crept into the tired old body as she began to tell others in the village about the wonderful God who had given her such peace and joy.

It was hard to believe that this could be the same woman who had begged for food from the missionaries' kitchen only a few years before.

One day Old One came to the missionaries' door. "Missesahibs," she called politely.

The new missionary hurried to the door. "Come in, Old One," she greeted her affectionately, glancing at the Bible the old woman carried in her hand. "Have you come to have someone read to you from God's Word?" she asked, for the old woman frequently sought out someone to read the Bible to her.

"Later . . ." Old One was bursting with important news that could not wait. "I have decided to go to school and learn to read the Bible myself," she announced proudly.

"To school?" The missionaries were stunned.

"Where?" they ventured, thinking of the Bible school at the mission and how impossible it would be to fit her into that schedule.

"There is a school in the next village where they teach old ones like me to read and write," the old woman answered. "I have learned of it, and I am going there. I can earn my food now. When I can read my Bible, I'll come back and tell others what it says."

"I believe you will!" the missionary replied with joy. "I truly believe you will."

3

THE MIRACLE OF THE WORD

"MIGUEL!" The bartender's voice rose above the babble of talking and laughter in the village *tambo* (crude saloon). "Your brother has passed out again. Take him home out of the way."

Miguel emptied his mug and went over to the inert form of Tomas sprawled on the floor. He pulled him to his feet and half-carried, half-dragged the drunken man up the path to his home. He dropped Tomas on a pallet in the corner of his hut. "Too bad," he said, shaking his head. He turned to Tomas's wife, Maria, "Do you have food?" he asked sympathetically, glancing at the thin children huddled in the corner.

"Some potatoes only," she said bitterly, searching the pockets of the inert man for a stray peso he might have missed.

Miguel sighed. "If only we could keep him away from the *tambo*. One drink and he can't stop." He turned to leave. "I have some beans," he added gruffly. "I'll bring you a sack." He went on down the path to his home.

It will take a miracle to change Tomas, he thought wearily, *and miracles don't happen today.*

But miracles sometimes do happen, and Miguel stumbled onto the beginning of one only a few days later.

It came about when he was coming home from a trip to the market. On the loneliest part of the mountain trail, Miguel was caught in a mountain rainstorm. He looked about anxiously for shelter. Half-hidden under a thorn tree he spied an abandoned adobe shanty.

He struggled through the soggy underbrush and crept inside. The building was dark and old, and no one had lived in it for a long time. But part of it was dry, and there was some protection from the icy wind. He huddled under his poncho and waited for the morning.

As the first light of the new day crept in through the broken door, Miguel looked up at the sagging roof of his shelter. Gradually his eyes made out an odd shape under the eaves. *What could that be?* he wondered. It looked like a package wrapped in brown paper. Could it be money or some other valuable loot hidden there long ago by a bandit and forgotten?

He straightened out his stiff, cramped legs and went to look closer. Gingerly he pulled the package from its hiding place and tore off the wrappings. It was only a book. Disappointed, he peered at the black cover. Across the top were faint, gilded letters. He spelled them out slowly, "S-A-N-T-A B-I-B-L-I-A."

"A Bible!" he muttered and dropped the Book as though it had scorched his fingers. He had never seen a Bible before, but he had been warned about it. This was the Book of the evangelicos. It was a sin to read it.

Miguel trembled as he sat on the ground in the hut, staring at the Book. He was curious. What strange words might be inside its covers? He remembered long ago hearing a man on the street in Chota say that the Bible contained the secret of a better life.

My brother Tomas could certainly profit by this secret, Miguel thought. *Do I dare to read it?*

He looked at the Book before him for a long time. *This may be my chance,* he thought. *I will take it home. Tonight when it is safe, I will open it and find out what it says.*

As soon as Miguel reached home, he hid the package where no one would see it. It would not do for anyone in the village to know he had a Bible.

When darkness fell and the villagers were all safely inside their own homes, Miguel lit his homemade lamp and sat down to read the Book. Cautiously he removed the brown wrapping. He spelled out the words slowly, syllable by syllable, stopping frequently to think about their meaning. As Miguel read, he became excited and troubled. *These things are not wicked,* he said to himself. *They are good. But if they are good, then the man in the market at Chota was right. The Bible tells us how to live better.*

This was something to think about a long time. If it was true, it could upset their whole lives. He continued to read and ponder.

After several weeks he talked to Tomas about the Book. "You ought to read it," Miguel urged. "It could make you a better man. Come by my house tonight and listen for yourself."

Tomas did stop by Miguel's home—at first fearfully, then with more and more interest. Miguel's wife, Luisa, worked about the house as the men read aloud. She said nothing, but she listened to the words and to the discussion of the men.

"This Book says good things," Tomas said at last. "But it also has things in it that I don't understand. I wish there was someone who could explain it."

"The evangelicos could explain it," Miguel said slowly, a little frightened by his boldness. "They have a chapel in Chota near the market, you know."

"But who would dare to venture inside that place?" Tomas asked.

Luisa listened, thought, and said nothing. She had heard enough to feel that the Book spoke the truth. She wished she could know more.

A few weeks later she heard the village women talking about a norteamericano missionary who was coming to the chapel of the evangelicos in Chota.

"Ha! A norteamericano come all the way up into the mountains to Chota?" she scoffed. "I don't believe it."

"Well, it's true," the talebearer insisted, nettled by Luisa's disdain. "My husband brought a piece of paper home from the market yesterday that told about it. He will be in Chota three weeks from last market day."

Luisa pretended not to hear her, but she counted the days carefully. On the right day she said to Miguel, "I'd like to go to market today. It has been more than a year since my mother died. It's time to begin wearing something colorful again."

"Sure, sure," Miguel teased. "You are always wanting to spend money. Do you have any?"

"Yes, a little," Luisa answered, smiling. She was glad he was in a pleasant mood.

"Very well, then," he said. "Put on your shawl, and we'll go."

They walked down the mountain trail, with Luisa carrying on her head the basket of vegetables they would sell in the market.

When the vegetables were sold, they strolled about the market seeing the wares of others. They were in no hurry to buy. At last Luisa found the cloth she wanted. She tucked her purchase inside her shawl, and they walked on.

"Let's go by the animal market," Luisa said after a time. "Maybe there will be a small guinea pig I can buy."

As they came near the white adobe church of the evangelicos, Luisa exclaimed, "Look at the crowd! I wonder what is going on."

They paused curiously at the open door, through which they plainly heard the voice of someone preaching.

"That's a stranger," Miguel said. "His Spanish is better than ours."

The pastor was standing at the church door and saw Miguel and Luisa listening at the gate.

He walked out to speak to them. "Won't you come in?" he invited.

Luisa looked eagerly at her husband. This was what she wanted very much to do. But Miguel stepped back, frightened.

The pastor realized the fear that filled his heart. He did not urge Miguel to come. He visited with them casually, talking about the weather, the market, and the prospects for a good harvest. Miguel listened guardedly.

At a pause in the conversation, the voice of the preacher came to them clearly.

"He speaks very good Spanish for a norteamericano, doesn't he?" the pastor said casually.

"A norteamericano?" Miguel asked curiously. "How did he get way up here in the mountains?"

"He lives on the coast, but we invited him to come and speak to us. He is very interesting. Wouldn't you like to step inside and hear him better? It is quite crowded, but I think there is a little room to stand just inside the door."

Luisa almost held her breath. Miguel was torn between fear and curiosity. He wanted to hear this norteamericano who spoke Spanish so fluently—but would he dare step inside the evangelicos' church? Surely in a crowd this large he would be safe.

Hesitantly he stepped forward. Luisa pressed close behind him so that he could not retreat. Trembling, Miguel climbed the few steps that led to the little church. He slid inside the door and looked around. The room was bare except for some benches and a platform where the norteamericano was speaking. He was holding a black book like the one Miguel had at home. People were sitting and standing everywhere.

As the norteamericano finished talking, he invited people to come to the front and ask God to forgive their sins.

Miguel was convinced that this man spoke the truth. He knew now that what he had read in the Bible was true. But he was afraid.

Pastor Garcia spoke to him gently. "Come, give your life to God, my friend," he urged. "He can forgive your sins and give you a new life. You can have peace in your heart."

Miguel wanted desperately to accept the invitation, but he could not bring himself to walk down the crowded aisle to the front.

Luisa waited anxiously. She wanted to pray, too, but she felt she could not pray unless Miguel did.

Pastor Garcia guessed why Miguel was hesitating. "Would you kneel right here where you are and ask God to forgive your sins?" he asked.

"Yes," Miguel answered, and he and Luisa knelt down by the door. The pastor prayed with them, and they opened their hearts to God. There were no tears. Quietly they followed the pastor's instructions, and as he quoted God's promises, they believed that God forgave them.

They rose from their knees and thanked the pastor for his kindness. Then they walked out the door and started home.

But though there had been no tears or words, there had been a wonderful change in their hearts.

"Tomas must hear of this," Miguel said. "This is just what he needs. Only God can deliver him from his drinking. We must get him to the evangelicos' chapel where he can hear about the Christ who can change his heart."

Tomas listened intently that night as Miguel explained what Christ had done for him and Luisa. It fitted exactly with what he had been reading in the Bible at Miguel's home.

"Can I believe now?" he asked.

"Yes," they both said, surprised and excited with his understanding. Then, as nearly as they remembered, they talked to him as the pastor had talked to them. And Tomas also confessed his sins and believed God meant what He had promised in the Bible to do.

It did not take long for the villagers to know that something had happened to Miguel and Tomas. The men were different. They no longer came to the *tambo* to drink. They were honest in their business transactions. They helped neighbors when they were in need. It was a marvel, but it made the villagers uncomfortable. They tried in every way possible to make Miguel and Tomas turn back to their old ways.

But in spite of their sneers, accusations, and sometimes violence, there was one thing no one could deny: Miguel and Tomas were different and better men.

Gradually, as their goodness impressed the people more deeply, the antagonism faded away. Men became ashamed to attack these two who did nothing but good.

Word filtered through the village that Miguel and Tomas studied the Bible in their homes. One at a time, under cover of darkness, a village man and sometimes his wife found an excuse to drop in to visit them. They stayed to listen to the reading of the Book. Some of the villagers found Christ for themselves. In a few years a little adobe chapel was built.

One day a man came from the coast to live among them and preach every Sunday in the chapel.

Thus the Word of God moved quietly through

the village of Chaupilanche [Chow-pee-LAN-chee] from edge to edge, and the lives of the village people will never be the same again.

MORE BOOKS BY HELEN TEMPLE

*W*ho would want to go and preach to a people for whom the slightest misstep could mean death? This is what God wanted Pastor J. C. Coetzer to do. *Strangers in the Land* tells the story of how Coetzer and his companion, Pastor Sentsho, entered the land of the Sekhukhune and how God began a great work among a fearsome people who were themselves gripped by their own dark fears.

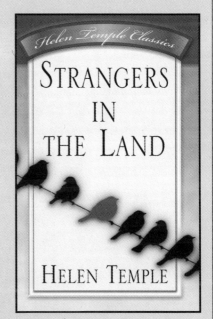

Helen Temple Classics

STRANGERS IN THE LAND

HELEN TEMPLE

*F*rom gripping suspense to tear-jerking drama, the three stories in *Shadow of His Wings* illustrate God's providential guidance and protection.

- A Muslim official finds more than he bargains for in his trip to a bazaar.
- A Chinese couple makes a daring escape from political oppression to freedom in Christ.
- A Japanese minister discovers God can bring forth life in the midst of death.

God has a purpose for all of His children. Find out what can happen when we put our lives in His hands.

BFZZ083-411-9587
To order call 1-800-877-0700 or E-mail orders@nph.com
Visit www.NPH.com

STORIES OUT OF AFRICA

Richard Zanner, who served two decades as Africa Regional Director for the Church of the Nazarene, experienced many adventures during his time in Africa. Take his all-night battle with a bat determined to share his hotel room, the sermon interrupted by a rifle-toting man coming down the aisle, the realization that his airplane had just barely missed a series of land mines placed on the runway, or an uncomfortable overnight trip with nomads on camelback. Read about one man's fascinating assortment of unusual mileposts in this intriguing book of testimonies to God's love, grace, and protection.

BFZZ083-411-9064
To order call 1-800-877-0700 or E-mail orders@nph.com
Visit www.NPH.com